STACEY DC

The Life and Times of a British Television
Presenter, Journalist, and Media Personality
from Humble Roots to Greatness

EDUVERSITY PRESS

Copyright

Copyright © 2024 Eduversity Press. All rights reserved. No part of this book may be reproduced, distributed, or transmitted in any form or by any means, including photocopying, recording, or other electronic or mechanical methods, without the prior written permission of the publisher, except in the case of brief quotations embodied in critical reviews and certain other noncommercial uses permitted by copyright law.

Table of Contents

Title Page

Copyright ii

Table of Contents iii

EPILOGUE 1

CHAPTER 1 5

EARLY LIFE 5

    Key Highlights 16

    Reflection Questions 18

CHAPTER 2 20

PROFESSIONAL CAREER 20

    2.1 Early Television Career (2008-2017) 20

    2.2 Rise to Prominence (2018-Present) 29

    Key Highlights 38

    Reflection Questions 40

CHAPTER 3 42

DOCUMENTARY WORK 42

Key Highlights 52

Reflection Questions 54

CHAPTER 4 .... **56**

PERSONAL LIFE **56**

Key Highlights 66

Reflection Questions 68

CHAPTER 5 .... **70**

CONTROVERSIES AND CHALLENGES .. **70**

Key Highlights 79

Reflection Questions 81

CHAPTER 6 .... **83**

AWARDS AND RECOGNITION **83**

Key Highlights 92

Reflection Questions 94

CHAPTER 7 .... **96**

LEGACY AND IMPACT **96**

Key Highlights 105

Reflection Questions 107

CHAPTER 8 109

FILMOGRAPHY 109

EPILOGUE 118

EPILOGUE

"Behind every great achievement lies an unlikely beginning." **Maya Angelou**

From the halls of London Airport to the global stage of investigative journalism, Stacey Dooley's story embodies the transformative power of passion, authenticity, and determination. Born on March 9, 1987, in Luton, Bedfordshire, few could have predicted that a shop assistant selling perfume would evolve into one of Britain's most respected documentary makers and broadcasters.

The journey began unexpectedly in 2008 when Dooley participated in BBC Three's "Blood, Sweat, and T-shirts." Her natural curiosity and genuine empathy for the garment workers she encountered in India distinguished her from other participants, catching the attention of BBC producers. This serendipitous moment launched a career that would reshape contemporary documentary journalism.

Her progression from participant to presenter proved remarkably swift. By 2009, "Stacey Dooley Investigates" hit the airwaves, beginning a series that would tackle some of the world's most pressing social issues. From child labor to sex trafficking, from environmental destruction to war zones, Dooley's distinctive approach brought complex global issues to mainstream audiences with unprecedented accessibility.

The year 2018 marked multiple milestones in her career. Her debut book, "On the Front Line with the Women Who Fight Back," became a Sunday Times bestseller, while her victory on "Strictly Come Dancing" with professional partner Kevin Clifton expanded her audience beyond news and documentary viewers. Most significantly, she received an MBE in the Birthday Honors for her services to broadcasting, validating her unique contribution to British television.

Beyond these achievements, Dooley's impact on broadcasting lies in her ability to connect with diverse audiences while maintaining journalistic integrity. Her work consistently demonstrates the ability to make serious subjects accessible without compromising their importance. This balance has proved particularly effective in engaging younger viewers with complex social issues.

Today, Stacey Dooley stands as a testament to the power of authentic storytelling and persistent dedication to truth. Her evolution from retail worker to decorated journalist, from documentary maker to versatile broadcaster, charts a course that inspires new generations of media professionals. This biography explores the remarkable journey of a woman who transformed herself and, in doing so, helped transform contemporary broadcasting.

Through triumphs and controversies, personal growth, and professional challenges, Dooley's story reminds us that greatness often emerges from unexpected beginnings. Her continuing influence on documentary journalism, social awareness, and public discourse demonstrates the lasting impact one authentic voice can have when guided by genuine passion for understanding and sharing human stories.

CHAPTER 1

EARLY LIFE

"Dreams don't work unless you do. I came from nothing, and that's what drives me every single day." **Stacey Dooley**

Born on March 9, 1987, in Luton, Bedfordshire, Stacey Jaclyn Dooley entered the world into circumstances that would shape her resilient character and determined spirit. The working-class town of Luton, known for its industrial heritage and diverse community, provided the backdrop for her formative years. Her early life story reflects the complexity of family dynamics that many British children faced in the late 1980s and early 1990s.

The departure of her Irish father when Stacey was merely two years old left an indelible mark on her childhood. His struggle with alcoholism and subsequent absence created a void that would influence her perspective on family relationships and personal responsibility. Her mother, who raised Stacey single-handedly, demonstrated remarkable strength and dedication, working tirelessly to provide for her daughter. This maternal influence instilled in young Stacey the values of hard work, perseverance, and independence that would later define her professional ethos.

Life in London during the 1990s presented its own set of challenges and opportunities. The family's modest means required careful budgeting and resourcefulness, teaching Stacey valuable lessons about financial management and appreciation for life's simple pleasures. Their home, though humble, was filled with love and encouragement, creating a nurturing environment despite economic constraints.

Stacey's education at Stopsley High School revealed both her potential and the limitations of her circumstances. The local comprehensive school, while providing basic education, didn't immediately suggest the pathway to media stardom that would later materialize. Her academic experience was marked by average performance rather than exceptional achievement, proving that traditional educational metrics don't always predict future success.

During her teenage years, Stacey encountered personal challenges that she would later discuss with characteristic honesty. She went through a brief phase of shoplifting with friends, a period she acknowledges as a misguided attempt to fit in and rebel against her circumstances. This chapter of her life, rather than defining her negatively, became a valuable lesson in accountability and personal growth.

The relationship with a drug dealer during her youth added another layer of complexity to her teenage experiences. Rather than glamorizing or hiding these aspects of her past, Stacey has used them to connect with young people facing similar challenges, demonstrating how early mistakes need not determine one's future path.

Her first steps into employment reflected the limited opportunities available to young people in Luton during the early 2000s. Working as a perfume saleswoman at Luton Airport might have seemed an unlikely launching pad for a future media career, but it provided valuable experience in customer service and human interaction. The role demanded quick thinking, adaptability, and the ability to connect with people from various backgrounds—skills that would prove invaluable in her later career.

The transition to working in a hairdressing salon in Bramingham represented another chapter in her early working life. The salon environment exposed her to different aspects of customer service and the art of conversation while also highlighting the limitations of local employment opportunities for ambitious young people with working-class backgrounds.

The absence of her father cast a long shadow over these formative years. His death during Stacey's twenties, before any possibility of reconciliation, brought a painful finality to their relationship. This loss, occurring just as she was beginning to establish herself professionally, added emotional depth to her understanding of human relationships and the importance of addressing personal issues before it's too late.

Financial struggles remained a constant companion during these early years. The necessity to contribute to household expenses while harboring dreams of a different future created a practical understanding of economic realities. This experience would later inform her documentary work on social issues and economic inequality.

The cultural landscape of Luton, with its diverse population and sometimes challenging social dynamics, provided Stacey with an early education in multiculturalism and social issues. Growing up in a town often misunderstood and misrepresented by national media helped develop her interest in telling stories from different perspectives.

Her mother's unwavering support during these challenging years proved crucial. Despite limited resources, she encouraged Stacey's ambitions and provided emotional stability. This maternal influence helped shape Stacey's approach to investigating stories about families and particularly women in difficult circumstances around the world.

Transportation between work and home often meant long bus rides through Luton's various neighborhoods, offering time for reflection and observation. These journeys through different communities contributed to her developing social awareness and interest in people's stories.

The local library became a sanctuary of sorts, offering free access to knowledge and entertainment. Here, Stacey discovered her love for storytelling and began to develop the curiosity that would later drive her documentary work. The hours spent reading magazines and newspapers planted the seeds for her future career in journalism.

Her early relationships with friends and colleagues in Luton helped develop her natural ability to connect with people from all walks of life. The authentic, straightforward communication style that would later become her trademark began taking shape during these formative years.

Personal health challenges, including managing stress and anxiety while navigating early adulthood, taught valuable lessons about self-care and mental health awareness. These experiences would later influence her approach to discussing sensitive topics in her documentaries.

The contrast between her early life experiences and her later success provides powerful testimony to the possibility of transcending circumstances through determination and hard work. Her journey from Luton's working-class environment to national television screens demonstrates the potential for social mobility through talent, persistence, and seizing opportunities.

Living through economic uncertainties in her early years developed her resilience and adaptability. The necessity to be resourceful and make the most of limited opportunities became valuable life skills that would serve her well in her future career.

Her early exposure to different social issues in Louisville, from economic disparity to cultural tensions, laid the groundwork for her later interest in investigative journalism. The town's complex social fabric provided firsthand experience of the issues she would later explore professionally.

The absence of privileged connections or inherited advantages meant that every step forward required determination and self-belief. This background would later help her maintain authenticity in her broadcasting career and connect with people from similar backgrounds.

Financial management became a necessary skill early in life. Learning to budget carefully and make ends meet provided practical experience that would later inform her understanding of economic issues in her documentary work.

The experience of working in customer-facing roles developed her natural ability to engage with people from different backgrounds. These early jobs, while modest in scope, helped build the communication skills essential for her future career in television.

Her relationship with education evolved beyond traditional academic metrics. While school provided basic skills, her real education came from observing and engaging with the world around her, developing the practical intelligence that would later distinguish her documentary work.

The impact of her father's absence and subsequent death contributed to her emotional intelligence and empathy, qualities that would become central to her interviewing style and approach to sensitive subjects in her documentaries.

Her early life in Luton, though challenging, provided rich material for understanding human nature and social dynamics. These experiences would later inform her approach to storytelling and investigation in her professional work.

The strong bond with her mother remained a constant source of support and inspiration, demonstrating the importance of family relationships in personal development and resilience. This understanding would later influence her treatment of family-related topics in her work.

Youth culture in Luton during the 1990s and early 2000s exposed her to various social issues and challenges facing young people. This firsthand experience would later help her connect with and understand youth-related issues in her documentary work.

The necessity to work from a young age instilled a strong work ethic and practical approach to life. These qualities would become valuable assets in building her career and maintaining professional standards in broadcasting.

Her early experiences with diversity in Luton developed her cultural awareness and sensitivity. This background would prove invaluable when producing documentaries about different cultures and social groups around the world.

The challenges of her youth, rather than limiting her potential, provided motivation and determination to pursue her ambitions. Her background became a source of strength rather than a barrier to success.

Key Highlights

1. Stacey's early family life was marked by her father's departure when she was two years old, leaving her mother to raise her singlehandedly in Luton. His struggle with alcoholism and eventual death before any reconciliation could occur deeply influenced her understanding of family dynamics and personal resilience.

2. Growing up in working-class Luton during the 1990s shaped Dooley's worldview significantly, with the local library becoming her sanctuary for learning and self-development. Despite limited resources, her mother's unwavering support and the diverse community around her helped forge her understanding of social issues and cultural differences.

3. Her teenage years presented considerable challenges, including a brief period of shoplifting and association with a drug dealer. Rather than hiding these experiences, Dooley later used them to connect authentically with others facing similar struggles, demonstrating how early mistakes need not define one's future.

4. Early employment as a perfume saleswoman at Luton Airport and later as a hairdresser in Birmingham provided valuable life lessons in human interaction and perseverance. These modest beginnings, while far from her future media career, developed her natural ability to connect with people from all walks of life—a skill that would prove invaluable in her later documentary work.

Reflection Questions

1. How might growing up with a single mother influence Stacey's drive for success?

   _____
   _____
   _____
   _____
   _____

2. What does Stacey's journey from teenage troubles to success teach us about second chances?

   _____
   _____
   _____
   _____
   _____

3. How did her early jobs shape her ability to connect with people in her documentaries?

　　_____

　　_____

　　_____

　　_____

　　_____

4. Why do you think being honest about her past matters to her work today?

　　_____

　　_____

　　_____

　　_____

　　_____

CHAPTER 2

PROFESSIONAL CAREER

"Television is not just about entertainment; it's about illuminating the human condition and giving voice to those who might otherwise go unheard."

David Attenborough

2.1 Early Television Career (2008-2017)

The year 2008 brought an unexpected twist to the life of a young shop assistant from Luton. Stacey Dooley, then working at the airport selling perfume, answered a casting call for a BBC Three documentary series titled "Blood, Sweat, and T-shirts." This decision would transform her from an ordinary retail worker into one of Britain's most respected documentary filmmakers.

"Blood, Sweat, and T-shirts" placed Dooley alongside other young fashion consumers in Indian garment factories, exposing them to the harsh realities of fast fashion production. While other participants focused on their personal discomfort, Dooley's genuine interest in the workers' lives and conditions set her apart. She asked thoughtful questions, showed genuine empathy, and demonstrated natural interviewing abilities that caught the attention of BBC producers.

Her performance on the show revealed an innate talent for connecting with people across cultural boundaries. The way she engaged with Indian garment workers, showing respect and genuine curiosity about their lives, demonstrated a rare ability to break down barriers and tell compelling human stories. BBC executives noticed her unique combination of approachability and journalistic instinct.

The success of her appearance led to a remarkable opportunity. BBC Three commissioned a series with Dooley as the presenter, launching "Stacey Dooley Investigates" in August 2009. The first episodes explored child labor in developing countries, a topic that resonated deeply with her experiences from "Blood, Sweat, and T-shirts." The series debut demonstrated her natural presenting style—direct yet compassionate, serious yet accessible.

2010 brought new challenges and opportunities with documentaries exploring increasingly complex subjects. Her investigation into child soldiers in the Democratic Republic of the Congo revealed her growing confidence in handling sensitive topics. The same year, she produced a powerful documentary about sex trafficking and underage sexual slavery in Cambodia, showcasing her ability to tackle difficult subjects while maintaining sensitivity and respect for them.

The development of her investigative style became evident through these early works. She perfected the art of asking tough questions without antagonizing her subjects, developing a distinctive approach that combined friendly accessibility with journalistic rigor. This style would become her trademark in subsequent years.

2011 saw Dooley expanding her repertoire with "Tourism and the Truth," a two-part series examining the impact of tourism on workers in Thailand and Kenya. The documentaries highlighted issues like wages, corruption, and environmental changes, demonstrating her growing expertise in connecting local stories to global issues.

Her work with young people took a new direction through the CBBC series "Show Me What You're Made Of," where she guided British children through experiences similar to her own in "Blood, Sweat, and T-shirts." This ability to adapt her presenting style for different audiences showcased her versatility as a broadcaster.

February 2012 brought a personal challenge when she filmed "My Hometown Fanatics" in Luton. The documentary required her to interview both Islamists and members of the English Defense League, testing her ability to maintain objectivity while reporting on issues close to home. Her balanced handling of this sensitive topic earned praise from critics and audiences alike.

The global financial crisis provided material for "Coming Here Soon," a three-part series broadcast in June and July 2012. Dooley traveled to Greece, Ireland, and Japan, examining how young people coped with economic upheaval. Though the Japan episode faced criticism for its coverage of suicide, it demonstrated her willingness to tackle controversial subjects.

Her growing reputation led to the creation of two series of "Stacey Dooley in the USA," where she investigated issues affecting American teenagers. From girls in juvenile detention to young people caught in border conflicts, these documentaries showcased her ability to tell compelling stories across cultural boundaries.

2015 represented a significant evolution in her documentary making with "Beaten By My Boyfriend." The investigation into domestic abuse within the UK demonstrated her maturity as a filmmaker and her skill in handling deeply personal stories with appropriate sensitivity and respect.

The following year brought new challenges with "Stacey Dooley in Cologne: The Blame Game," examining the 2015 New Year's Eve sexual assaults in Germany. Her coverage of the Orlando Pulse Bar shootings in "Stacey Dooley: Hate and Pride in Orlando" further demonstrated her ability to report on breaking news events while maintaining her characteristic sensitivity.

November 2016 saw the release of "Brainwashing Stacey," where she immersed herself in controversial environments, including an American anti-abortion summer camp and African big-game hunters. These experiences tested her ability to maintain professional objectivity while confronting views that challenged her personal beliefs.

Her dedication to uncovering difficult stories led to a dangerous situation in Tokyo while filming "Young Sex For Sale in Japan." The two-hour detention by local police, following a confrontation with men protecting exploited girls, highlighted the risks she was willing to take to expose important stories.

2017 brought new challenges with "Canada's Lost Girls," investigating the disappearance and murder of over 1,200 Indigenous women. This documentary showcased her evolution as a journalist, handling complex historical and social issues with depth and sensitivity. Her narration of "The Natives: This Is Our America" further demonstrated her ability to give voice to marginalized communities.

Throughout these years, Dooley developed a distinctive documentary style characterized by direct questioning, genuine empathy, and a commitment to highlighting underreported stories.

Her work consistently demonstrated the value of allowing subjects to tell their own stories while providing necessary context for viewers.

Her international documentary work took her to some of the world's most challenging environments. From war zones to sites of environmental destruction, she maintained her commitment to telling important stories while ensuring the safety and dignity of her subjects.

The evolution of her career from 2008 to 2017 demonstrates the development of a significant voice in British broadcasting. Her ability to combine serious journalism with accessible presentation helped create a new model for documentary filmmaking, particularly in reaching younger audiences.

These early years established her reputation for tackling difficult subjects with sensitivity and determination. Her work consistently challenged viewers' preconceptions while maintaining high standards of journalistic integrity and ethical reporting.

The diversity of topics she covered during this period—from fashion industry exploitation to religious extremism, from youth crime to environmental destruction—showed her versatility as a documentary maker. Each project added new dimensions to her skillset and reputation.

Her success in this period came from an ability to balance serious journalism with personal warmth. She maintained professional standards while allowing her natural personality to engage viewers and subjects alike, creating documentaries that informed and connected with audiences on an emotional level.

This period of her career demonstrated the value of authentic storytelling in documentary making. Her background and natural approach helped her connect with subjects from all walks of life, creating trust that allowed for more honest and revealing interviews.

The range of her work during these years established her as more than just a presenter; she became a respected voice in British journalism, known for tackling difficult subjects with courage and compassion. Her journey from retail worker to award-winning documentary maker inspires others from similar backgrounds.

2.2 Rise to Prominence (2018-Present)

The year 2018 transformed Stacey Dooley from a respected documentary maker into a household name across Britain. Her announcement as the eighth contestant for the sixteenth series of Strictly Come Dancing surprised many who knew her primarily for serious journalism. The decision to join the popular entertainment show demonstrated her versatility and willingness to step outside her comfort zone.

Dancing alongside professional partner Kevin Clifton, Dooley revealed a natural grace and determination that resonated with viewers. Their partnership proved magical, combining technical skill with genuine chemistry that captured the public's imagination. Week after week, they delivered memorable performances, showing steady improvement and dedication to mastering each dance style.

The journey through Strictly challenged Dooley physically and emotionally, pushing her beyond the boundaries of her previous experiences. Her work ethic, honed through years of documentary making, served her well during the grueling training schedule. The transformation from nervous beginner to confident performer mirrored her professional evolution from shop assistant to celebrated journalist.

December 15, 2018, saw Dooley and Clifton crowned champions of Strictly Come Dancing. Their victory represented more than just dancing excellence; it symbolized the triumph of hard work, perseverance, and authentic personality. The win elevated her public profile significantly, introducing her to audiences who might not have encountered her documentary work.

Earlier that same year, Dooley achieved another significant milestone with the publication of her first book, "On the Front Line with the Women Who Fight Back." The book, which became a Sunday Times bestseller, showcased her commitment to highlighting women's stories and struggles worldwide. Through compelling narratives and personal reflections, she brought attention to issues ranging from sex trafficking to domestic violence.

Recognition of her contributions to broadcasting came with the appointment as Member of the Order of the British Empire (MBE) in the 2018 Birthday Honours. This prestigious award acknowledged her dedication to uncovering important stories and giving voice to the voiceless. The honor reflected both her professional achievements and her impact on British television.

Following her strict success, Dooley's television career expanded in new directions. The BBC appointed her co-presenter of New Year Live on BBC One alongside fellow Strictly contestant Joe Sugg. This mainstream entertainment role demonstrated her ability to balance serious journalism with lighter presenting duties.

2019 brought fresh opportunities and challenges. Her appointment as Grazia's contributing editor for investigations added print journalism to her growing portfolio. The role allowed her to reach new audiences while maintaining her focus on investigating important social issues.

The launch of BBC Three's reality competition series "Glow Up: Britain's Next Make-Up Star" showcased another facet of her presenting abilities. Leading this creative competition required different skills from her documentary work, proving her versatility as a broadcaster. Her warm, encouraging approach to contestants balanced well with the show's competitive nature.

Television appearances multiplied, including guest judging on RuPaul's Drag Race UK and presenting The One Show. Each role allowed Dooley to develop her presenting style while maintaining the authenticity that had characterized her documentary work.

Documentary making remained central to her work. "Stacey Meets the IS Brides" and "Stacey Dooley: Face to Face with the Bounty Hunters" demonstrated her continued commitment to serious journalism. These programs became the most-watched documentaries on BBC iPlayer, confirming her ability to attract viewers to challenging subjects.

2020 saw Dooley expanding her repertoire further, appearing in Jessie Ware's music video for "Save a Kiss" and participating in Michael McIntyre's The Wheel. These entertainment appearances helped maintain her public profile while she continued producing serious documentaries.

The launch of "DNA Family Secrets" in 2021 partnered her with geneticist Turi King, helping people solve family mysteries through genetic testing. This series combined human interest stories with scientific discovery, showcasing her ability to make complex subjects accessible to general audiences.

Her participation in various television formats continued with appearances on celebrity game shows and panel programs. Each appearance reinforced her status as a versatile broadcaster capable of handling both entertainment and serious programming.

Throughout this period, Dooley maintained her commitment to documentary making while embracing new challenges. Her work consistently demonstrated an ability to connect with audiences across different formats and subjects. The balance between serious journalism and entertainment work helped build a broader platform for her social justice messages.

The announcement of her stage debut in "2:22 A Ghost Story" at London's Gielgud Theatre marked another bold step in her career evolution. Taking on the role of Jenny demonstrated her willingness to challenge herself professionally and explore new forms of storytelling.

Personal developments during this period also influenced her public persona. Her relationship with Kevin Clifton, which began after their Strictly partnership, added new dimensions to her public profile. Their announcement of expecting a baby in 2022 and the birth of their daughter in 2023 showed another side of her life to the public.

These years of rising prominence saw Dooley successfully balancing multiple aspects of her career while maintaining the authenticity that had characterized her early work. Her ability to move between serious documentaries and entertainment programming without losing credibility demonstrated rare professional versatility.

The evolution from documentary maker to multi-faceted media personality brought new opportunities and challenges. Each new role required different skills while maintaining the genuine approach that had endeared her to audiences. Her success across various formats proved that authenticity and hard work could translate across different media contexts.

Book publishing added another dimension to her career. The success of her first book led to further writing projects, allowing her to explore topics in greater depth than television formats permitted. These works provided platforms for examining social issues while sharing personal insights from her experiences.

Throughout her rise to prominence, Dooley maintained connections with her documentary roots while embracing new opportunities. This balance helped establish her as a trusted voice across multiple platforms and formats. Her journey from focused documentary maker to versatile broadcaster demonstrated the value of staying true to one's principles while remaining open to new challenges.

The recognition of her work through awards and honors validated her approach to broadcasting. Beyond the MBE, she received various industry accolades acknowledging both her journalism and entertainment work. These honors reflected her impact on British television and her role in making serious subjects accessible to wider audiences.

Stage work represented the newest frontier in her career development. The challenge of live theater added another dimension to her performing abilities, requiring different skills from television presenting or documentary making. This willingness to step into unfamiliar territory exemplified her approach to professional growth.

Her expansion into different media formats never came at the expense of her commitment to social issues. Each new platform provided opportunities to reach different audiences with important messages.

Key Highlights

1. Stacey Dooley's television breakthrough began with "Blood, Sweat, and T-shirts" in 2008, leading to her own series, "Stacey Dooley Investigates." Her natural ability to connect with subjects and tackle challenging topics established her as a respected documentary filmmaker, covering issues from child labor to sex trafficking across multiple countries.

2. The year 2018 marked a transformative period in her career with three major achievements: winning Strictly Come Dancing with Kevin Clifton, publishing her Sunday Times bestseller "On the Front Line with the Women Who Fight Back," and receiving an MBE in the Birthday Honours for services to broadcasting.

3. Following her Strictly success, Dooley successfully diversified her career, balancing serious documentary work with entertainment roles including hosting "Glow Up: Britain's Next Make-Up Star," presenting BBC's The One Show, and guest judging on RuPaul's Drag Race UK, while maintaining her credibility as a journalist.

4. Her professional evolution culminated in new ventures including the DNA Family Secrets series, multiple television presenting roles, and her stage debut in "2:22 A Ghost Story," demonstrating her versatility across different media formats while staying true to her documentary-making roots.

Reflection Questions

1. How did Stacey's authentic presenting style help her transition from serious documentaries to entertainment shows while maintaining her credibility?

   _____
   _____
   _____
   _____
   _____

2. What role did taking risks, like joining Strictly Come Dancing, play in transforming her career pursuit?

   _____
   _____
   _____
   _____
   _____

3. How has Stacey managed to balance entertainment roles with serious journalism while staying true to her values?

___
___
___
___
___

4. In what ways has her personal background helped her connect with diverse audiences across different media formats?

___
___
___
___
___

CHAPTER 3

DOCUMENTARY WORK

"The camera is an instrument that teaches people how to see without a camera." **Dorothea Lange**

True documentary filmmaking requires more than just pointing a camera and asking questions. Through her extensive body of work, Stacey Dooley has demonstrated an exceptional ability to shine light on complex social issues while maintaining dignity and respect for her subjects. Her documentary portfolio spans continents, cultures, and controversial topics, creating a powerful legacy of storytelling and social impact.

The foundation of Dooley's documentary work rests on her coverage of pressing social issues. Her series "Tourism and the Truth" exposed the hidden costs of global tourism, revealing how local communities in Thailand and Kenya struggle with exploitation and environmental degradation. The documentary went beyond surface-level analysis, examining the complex relationships between tourism operators, local workers, and international visitors.

Child exploitation emerged as a recurring theme in her investigations. The groundbreaking documentary "Kids for Sale" exposed the dark reality of child labor in sweatshops across developing nations. Through careful storytelling and sensitive interviewing techniques, Dooley brought viewers face-to-face with the human cost of fast fashion and consumer culture.

Her investigation into sex trafficking took her to multiple countries, resulting in powerful documentaries that revealed the global scale of this crisis. "Young Sex for Sale in Japan" required particular courage, leading to a confrontation with local authorities while investigating the exploitation of underage girls in Tokyo's entertainment districts.

The documentary "Face to Face with ISIS" demonstrated Dooley's willingness to tackle dangerous subjects. Meeting with ISIS fighters and their families required extraordinary preparation and bravery. The resulting film provided rare insights into the mindset of extremists while highlighting the impact of terrorism on local communities.

International investigations became a hallmark of her work. "Russia's War on Women" exposed domestic violence issues in a country where such discussions remain taboo. Through careful relationship building and persistent questioning, Dooley gained access to stories that might otherwise have remained hidden.

"Coming Here Soon" examined the impact of economic crises across different cultures. From Greece to Ireland to Japan, Dooley documented how young people coped with financial uncertainty and social change. These documentaries highlighted common traits in human experience while respecting cultural differences.

The award-winning "Stacey Dooley: Face to Face with ISIS" received the Popular Features Award at the One World Media Awards in 2018. This recognition acknowledged not only the documentary's journalistic merit but also its contribution to public understanding of complex global issues.

"Canada's Lost Girls" brought attention to the disappearance and murder of Indigenous women, earning critical acclaim for its sensitive handling of historical trauma and ongoing injustice. The documentary combined historical research with contemporary investigation, creating a powerful narrative about systemic discrimination and violence.

Notable series like "Stacey Dooley Investigates" consistently tackled difficult subjects while maintaining high production values and ethical standards. Episodes covering topics from mental health to environmental destruction demonstrated her range as a documentarian and her commitment to thorough research.

The series "Sex in Strange Places" explored different cultural attitudes toward sexuality and sex work. Though controversial, these documentaries maintained professional standards while examining complex social and ethical questions. Dooley's approach allowed subjects to share their stories without judgment or sensationalism.

Her work on domestic violence resulted in "Beaten By My Boyfriend," a powerful examination of relationship abuse in the UK. This documentary proved particularly impactful by bringing attention to issues often hidden within seemingly normal relationships.

"My Hometown Fanatics" demonstrated her ability to maintain objectivity while covering personally challenging topics. Returning to Luton to investigate religious extremism required careful balance between professional distance and personal connection to the community.

The success of these documentaries relied heavily on Dooley's distinctive interviewing style. Her ability to ask difficult questions while showing genuine empathy allowed subjects to open up about traumatic experiences and controversial opinions. This approach created trust and enabled deeper exploration of complex issues.

Environmental documentaries like "Fashion's Dirty Secrets" exposed the ecological impact of consumer culture. These programs combined scientific evidence with human stories, making abstract environmental issues concrete and relatable for viewers.

Her work frequently highlighted women's stories and struggles. From war zones to fashion factories, Dooley consistently sought out female voices and experiences often overlooked by mainstream media. This focus contributed significantly to public understanding of gender-based issues globally.

The documentary series "Stacey Dooley Sleeps Over" took a different approach, embedding herself in unusual households to understand different lifestyles and belief systems. This format allowed for intimate exploration of social issues through personal stories and daily experiences.

Mental health became another important focus, with documentaries examining psychiatric care and treatment facilities. These sensitive productions helped reduce stigma while highlighting both challenges and innovations in mental health care.

Her investigation of youth issues spans multiple continents and contexts. From child soldiers in Congo to teenage inmates in American prisons, these documentaries gave voice to young people caught in difficult circumstances. The resulting body of work provides valuable insights into global youth culture and challenges.

Drug-related documentaries required particular care to avoid sensationalism while maintaining journalistic integrity. Programs examining both users and law enforcement perspectives contributed to public understanding of complex policy issues.

Special investigations into human trafficking networks demonstrated both journalistic courage and careful attention to victim protection. These documentaries helped raise awareness while respecting the dignity and safety of vulnerable subjects.

The evolution of her documentary style shows increasing sophistication in handling complex subjects. Early works focused primarily on direct investigation, while later productions incorporated broader context and multiple perspectives.

Her coverage of war zones and conflict areas produced powerful testimony about the human cost of violence. These documentaries required careful preparation and risk assessment while maintaining journalistic standards under challenging conditions.

The impact of her documentary work extends beyond television audiences. Many programs have been used in educational settings and by advocacy groups to raise awareness about social issues. This educational legacy demonstrates the lasting value of quality documentary journalism.

Recent productions have increasingly incorporated new storytelling techniques while maintaining focus on important social issues. Innovation in format and presentation helps reach new audiences while preserving the core mission of investigative journalism.

Throughout her documentary career, Dooley has maintained high ethical standards while tackling controversial subjects. This commitment to responsible journalism while covering challenging topics has earned respect from both colleagues and subjects.

The collection of awards and recognition for her documentary work validates both her approach and impact. Beyond specific honors, the consistent quality and integrity of her productions have established new standards for social issue documentaries.

Her body of work creates a valuable historical record of social issues in the early 21st century. Future viewers will find in these documentaries a thoughtful examination of key challenges facing contemporary society.

The lasting influence of her documentary style can be seen in new generations of journalists and filmmakers. Her approach to sensitive subjects while maintaining both professionalism and humanity provides a model for responsible documentary making.

Key Highlights

1. Stacey Dooley's documentary portfolio showcases her fearless approach to investigating challenging social issues, from child exploitation and sex trafficking to her face-to-face encounters with ISIS fighters, consistently maintaining dignity and respect for her subjects while exposing difficult truths.

2. Her international investigations have taken her across the globe, producing powerful documentaries like "Russia's War on Women," "Canada's Lost Girls," and "Young Sex for Sale in Japan," often requiring extraordinary courage while tackling dangerous and controversial subjects.

3. The success of her award-winning productions, particularly "Face to Face with ISIS," which won the Popular Features Award at the One World Media Awards, demonstrates her ability to combine journalistic excellence with compelling storytelling while maintaining high ethical standards.

4. Through notable series like "Stacey Dooley Investigates" and "Stacey Dooley Sleeps Over," she developed a distinctive interviewing style that combines tough questioning with genuine empathy, allowing her to tackle complex subjects from mental health to environmental issues while making them accessible to mainstream audiences.

Reflection Questions

1. How has Dooley's approach to interviewing vulnerable subjects shaped the way sensitive stories are told in documentary journalism?

2. What role does empathy play in her ability to investigate difficult topics while maintaining subjects' dignity?

3. How has her documentary work influenced public understanding of global social issues?

_____

_____

_____

_____

_____

4. Why do you think Dooley's style of combining tough journalism with genuine compassion resonates with audiences?

_____

_____

_____

_____

_____

CHAPTER 4

PERSONAL LIFE

"Love and work are the cornerstones of our humanness." **Sigmund Freud**

Behind every public figure lies a private world that shapes their character and influences their professional journey. For Stacey Dooley, the intersection of personal life and career created a narrative that resonates with many who follow her story. Her relationship with Kevin Clifton, journey into motherhood, and passionate advocacy work reveal dimensions of her character beyond the documentary maker's lens.

The story of Stacey and Kevin began on the dance floor of Strictly Dancing in 2018. Their partnership quickly demonstrated chemistry that transcended mere performance, though both maintained professional boundaries throughout the competition. Their eventual victory in December 2018 marked not only a professional triumph but laid the foundation for a deeper connection.

Early 2019 brought news of their romantic relationship, capturing public attention and media interest. The transition from dance partners to life partners unfolded naturally, with both Stacey and Kevin approaching their relationship with the same authenticity that characterized their professional work. They navigated public scrutiny while maintaining privacy around their personal connection.

Their shared appreciation for performing arts and storytelling created a strong foundation for their relationship. Kevin's background in dance and theater complemented Stacey's documentary work, each understanding the demands and rewards of creative professions. This mutual understanding helped them support each other's careers while building their lives together.

The couple's approach to public life demonstrated thoughtful balance. They shared glimpses of their relationship through social media and interviews while maintaining boundaries that protected their private world. This careful navigation of public interest reflected their understanding of fame's double-edged nature.

August 2022 brought joyful news when Stacey announced her pregnancy via Instagram. The announcement reflected their characteristic style: personal yet measured, sharing happiness while maintaining privacy. Their decision to share this milestone with their audience demonstrated the authentic connection they maintained with supporters.

Preparation for parenthood revealed new aspects of both their characters. Stacey continued working on documentaries during her pregnancy, demonstrating her commitment to professional responsibilities while embracing this personal transformation. Their approach to impending parenthood reflected careful consideration of how to balance family life with public careers.

January 2023 welcomed their daughter, marking the beginning of a new chapter in their lives. Parenthood brought changes to their professional rhythms and personal priorities, with both parents adapting their careers to accommodate family life. Their experience reflected challenges familiar to many working parents: navigating childcare, career demands, and personal fulfillment.

Motherhood influenced Stacey's perspective on many issues she covered in her documentaries. Personal experience with pregnancy and childbirth deepened her understanding of women's issues globally. This new dimension added richness to her reporting on topics affecting mothers and children worldwide.

The couple's parenting philosophy emphasized privacy for their child while maintaining their professional commitments. They chose to limit public exposure to their daughter, protecting her right to develop away from media attention. This decision reflected careful consideration of how to balance public careers with private family life.

Beyond her immediate family relationships, Stacey's personal views and advocacy work reveal a deep commitment to social justice. Her feminist perspective shapes both professional projects and personal statements, consistently supporting women's rights and gender equality. These values influence her choice of documentary subjects and public statements.

Environmental advocacy became increasingly important in her personal and professional life. Her investigations into fashion industry pollution led to changes in her own consumer habits, demonstrating commitment to practicing principles she promotes through her work. This consistency between personal choices and public advocacy strengthens her credibility on environmental issues.

Mental health awareness features prominently in her advocacy work. Personal openness about stress management and emotional wellbeing helps reduce stigma around mental health discussions. Her willingness to share personal experiences while maintaining appropriate boundaries provides a model for public figures addressing sensitive topics.

Social media presence reflects a careful balance between personal expression and professional responsibility. She uses platforms to highlight important issues while sharing select personal moments, maintaining authenticity without overexposure. This approach demonstrates understanding of social media's role in modern public life.

Educational advocacy remains central to her public role. Support for opportunities that helped her own career development shows commitment to expanding access for others from similar backgrounds. Her personal story serves as inspiration while her advocacy works toward systemic change.

Housing rights and economic justice feature among the causes she supports personally and professionally. Understanding of these issues stems from early life experiences, informing both documentary work and private advocacy. Personal connection to these challenges strengthens her ability to communicate their importance.

LGBTQ+ rights receive consistent support through both public statements and professional projects. This advocacy reflects broader commitment to human rights and dignity for all people. Personal support for these causes complements professional coverage of related issues.

Religious and cultural tolerance form important elements of her personal philosophy. Experience reporting from diverse communities worldwide influences her approach to interfaith and intercultural dialogue. These values shape both personal interactions and professional projects.

Consumer ethics and responsible shopping practices reflect personal commitment to social justice through daily choices. An investigation of fashion industry conditions influenced personal shopping habits, demonstrating a connection between professional knowledge and personal behavior.

Youth empowerment particularly resonates given her own journey from teenage years to public figure. Support for young people facing challenges similar to her early experiences shows understanding of obstacles and opportunities facing new generations.

Immigration and refugee rights feature among causes receiving personal support alongside professional coverage. Direct experience reporting from affected communities influences personal advocacy on these issues. Understanding gained through documentary work informs personal positions.

Gender-based violence prevention represents the intersection of personal conviction and professional expertise. Documentation of these issues worldwide strengthens commitment to supporting prevention and support services. Personal advocacy complements professional coverage of these crucial topics.

Workers' rights and fair labor practices remain important personal causes, reflecting early career experiences and subsequent investigations. Support for improved working conditions demonstrates consistency between personal values and professional focus.

Digital rights and online safety increasingly feature in both personal advocacy and professional work. Understanding technology's impact on society influences approach to these emerging issues. Personal interest in these topics shapes the selection of related documentary subjects.

Environmental sustainability practices extend beyond professional coverage into personal lifestyle choices. Commitment to reducing environmental impact shows through daily decisions and public advocacy. Personal choices reflect professional understanding of environmental challenges.

Child welfare advocacy stems from both professional expertise and personal concern for future generations. Support for child protection initiatives demonstrates a connection between documentary subjects and personal values. Professional investigation of these issues strengthens personal commitment to supporting solutions.

Key Highlights

1. The relationship between Stacey Dooley and Kevin Clifton blossomed from their Strictly Come Dancing partnership in 2018, evolving from professional dancers to life partners, with both successfully balancing their public careers while maintaining personal privacy.

2. Their journey into parenthood, marked by the announcement of Stacey's pregnancy in August 2022 and the birth of their daughter in January 2023, brought new dimensions to their lives while influencing Stacey's perspective on many of the issues she covers in her documentaries.

3. Stacey's personal advocacy work spans multiple causes, including feminism, environmental sustainability, mental health awareness, and social justice, with her own

experiences informing both her documentary work and public statements.

4. She maintains a thoughtful balance between sharing personal life moments and protecting private boundaries, particularly regarding her family life, while using her platform to advocate for causes she believes in, demonstrating consistency between her personal values and professional work.

Reflection Questions

1. How has Stacey's relationship with Kevin Clifton influenced her approach to balancing public life and private happiness?

   _____
   _____
   _____
   _____
   _____

2. In what ways has motherhood shaped her perspective on the social issues she covers in her documentaries?

   _____
   _____
   _____
   _____
   _____

3. How does Stacey's personal advocacy work reflect the values she demonstrates in her professional life?

4. Why do you think Stacey's approach to sharing personal life while maintaining boundaries resonates with her audience?

CHAPTER 5

CONTROVERSIES AND CHALLENGES

"The truth is rarely pure and never simple."
Oscar Wilde

Public figures who tackle challenging subjects inevitably face criticism and controversy. For Stacey Dooley, two significant controversies tested her professional reputation and sparked broader discussions about journalistic responsibility and representation in media.

The Turkish documentary episode of "Sex in Strange Places" became a focal point of criticism in January 2019. The controversy centered on the misidentification of a Turkish woman who was incorrectly portrayed as a Syrian sex worker living in Istanbul. This error led to immediate backlash from viewers and critics, highlighting issues of fact-checking and representation in documentary filmmaking.

BBC Three responded by removing the episode from iPlayer, acknowledging the serious nature of the misrepresentation. The incident raised questions about verification processes and the responsibility of filmmakers when portraying vulnerable individuals. Critics pointed to the potential harm such misidentification could cause to both the individual involved and the broader communities being represented.

The controversy prompted discussions within the media industry about documentary-making practices and the importance of thorough fact-checking. Professional journalists and documentary makers examined their own procedures, using this incident as a case study in the challenges of international reporting.

Dooley's response to the Turkish documentary criticism demonstrated professional accountability. Rather than becoming defensive, she acknowledged the error and supported the decision to remove the episode. This approach helped maintain her credibility while contributing to important discussions about journalistic standards.

However, a more significant controversy emerged in February 2019 during Dooley's work with Comic Relief in Uganda. The publication of photographs showing her holding a Ugandan child sparked intense debate about "white savior" narratives in charitable fundraising. British MP David Lammy publicly criticized the images, arguing they perpetuated unhelpful stereotypes about Africa.

The ensuing social media storm brought attention to long-standing concerns about how Western media portrays developing nations.

Ugandan campaign group No White Saviours joined the criticism, highlighting the need for different approaches to international charity work and representation.

Media coverage of the controversy extended beyond social media, with mainstream news outlets exploring broader questions about charitable campaigns and representation. The Guardian columnist Gaby Hinsliff noted how celebrity involvement in charity work had begun to feel increasingly problematic, particularly regarding the overshadowing of local voices.

The public response divided between those supporting traditional charitable approaches and others calling for fundamental changes in how Western organizations represent African communities. This division reflected deeper societal discussions about colonialism's legacy and contemporary international development practices.

Dooley maintained her position, stating she had no regrets about the incident while engaging thoughtfully with the criticism. Her response balanced defending her intentions with acknowledging the importance of the broader discussion about representation and narrative control.

The controversy's impact reached beyond individual reputations. Comic Relief founder Richard Curtis later announced changes to the charity's approach, telling Parliament they would stop sending celebrities abroad. This organizational shift demonstrated how public discourse could influence institutional practices.

Professional observers noted how the controversy highlighted evolving public attitudes toward international charity work. The incident became a reference point for discussions about changing approaches to humanitarian storytelling and representation.

The broader media industry responded by examining practices around international reporting and charitable campaigns. Publications and organizations began reviewing their approaches to similar content, considering how to maintain

74

emotional engagement while avoiding problematic narratives.

Industry professionals used these controversies to develop new guidelines for international reporting and representation. The incidents contributed to ongoing discussions about ethical storytelling and the responsibility of media makers toward their subjects.

Both controversies revealed the complex challenges facing documentary makers in an increasingly connected world. The incidents highlighted tensions between traditional storytelling approaches and evolving social consciousness about representation and power dynamics.

The public impact extended beyond immediate media coverage. Educational institutions incorporated these cases into journalism and media studies curricula, using them to explore ethical considerations in contemporary reporting.

Professional organizations examined their guidelines for international reporting and documentary making. The controversies contributed to developing new standards for representing communities and individuals in media projects. The long-term effects of these controversies shaped subsequent approaches to similar projects. Media organizations became more mindful of representation issues and more careful about verification procedures in international reporting. Documentaries featuring international subjects faced increased scrutiny following these incidents. Producers and broadcasters implemented additional checks and balances to prevent similar controversy. The discussion sparked by these controversies contributed to a broader social dialogue about media representation and responsibility. Public awareness of these issues increased, leading to more informed consumption of documentary content.

Media literacy educators used these cases to help students understand complex issues of representation and responsibility in journalism. The controversies became valuable teaching tools for exploring ethical considerations in media production.

Industry professionals developed new approaches to storytelling that maintained emotional impact while avoiding problematic representations. These innovations demonstrated how controversy could lead to positive changes in professional practice.

The response to these controversies revealed evolving public expectations for media accountability. Audiences demanded more thorough fact-checking and more thoughtful approaches to representation in documentary work.

Professional development programs incorporated lessons learned from these incidents into their training materials. New generations of documentary makers studied these cases to understand the importance of careful verification and responsible representation.

The controversies contributed to ongoing discussions about power dynamics in international media production. Industry professionals examined their roles in shaping global narratives and representing diverse communities. These incidents highlighted the challenges of maintaining journalistic integrity while working under pressure to produce compelling content. The discussion helped develop better practices for balancing these competing demands.

The public discourse surrounding these controversies demonstrated increasing sophistication in media criticism. Audiences showed greater awareness of representation issues and higher expectations for ethical reporting.

Professional relationships between media organizations and charitable institutions evolved following these incidents. New protocols developed for collaborations between broadcasters and nonprofit organizations.

The long-term impact of these controversies continues to influence approaches to international documentary making and charitable campaigns.

Key Highlights

1. The controversy surrounding Stacey Dooley's Turkish documentary "Sex in Strange Places" highlighted serious issues of misrepresentation when a Turkish woman was incorrectly portrayed as a Syrian sex worker, leading to the episode's removal from BBC iPlayer and sparking discussions about journalistic verification processes.

2. A significant debate erupted in February 2019 when photos of Dooley holding a Ugandan child during her Comic Relief work drew criticism from MP David Lammy and the Ugandan campaign group No White Saviours, igniting discussions about "white savior" narratives in charitable fundraising.

3. The Comic Relief controversy led to substantial organizational change, with founder Richard Curtis announcing they

would stop sending celebrities abroad, demonstrating how public discourse can influence institutional practices in charitable organizations.

4. These controversies contributed to broader industry changes, sparking new discussions about ethical storytelling, media representation, and the development of improved guidelines for international reporting and documentary making.

Reflection Questions

1. How did the Turkish documentary controversy change our understanding of fact-checking responsibilities in international reporting?

   _____
   _____
   _____
   _____
   _____

2. What does the Comic Relief debate reveal about changing attitudes toward charitable representation in media?

   _____
   _____
   _____
   _____
   _____

3. How might these controversies have shaped Stacey's approach to documentary making and representation?

4. Why do you think these incidents sparked such significant changes in both media and charitable organizations?

CHAPTER 6

AWARDS AND RECOGNITION

"Recognition is the greatest motivator."
Gerard C. Eakedale

The journey from shop assistant to decorated journalist represents a remarkable story of talent, determination, and impact. Stacey Dooley's collection of awards and honors reflects not just personal achievement but the broader significance of her contributions to broadcasting and journalism.

The 2018 Birthday Honours brought the most prestigious recognition of her career when Dooley was appointed Member of the Order of the British Empire (MBE). This honor, bestowed by Queen Elizabeth II, acknowledged her outstanding services to broadcasting. The ceremony at Buckingham Palace celebrated her dedication to uncovering important stories and giving voice to marginalized communities worldwide.

The MBE recognition held particular significance given Dooley's background. Her path from Luton Airport's perfume counter to receiving one of Britain's highest honors demonstrated the transformative power of dedication and authenticity in journalism. The award validated her distinctive approach to documentary making, combining serious investigation with accessible presentation.

Recognition from her peers came through numerous industry accolades. The One World Media Awards celebrated her groundbreaking work with ISIS survivors, honoring "Face to Face with ISIS" in their Popular Features category. This award particularly acknowledged her ability to handle sensitive subjects while maintaining journalistic integrity.

BBC Three's viewership records fell repeatedly to Dooley's documentaries. Her investigations consistently ranked among the most watched programs on BBC iPlayer, demonstrating both critical acclaim and popular appeal. These viewing figures validated her ability to attract audiences to challenging subjects.

Professional organizations regularly sought her expertise, inviting her to judge prestigious competitions and speak at industry events. The Royal Television Society recognized her contributions through multiple nominations, acknowledging her impact on contemporary broadcast journalism.

Her documentary "Young Sex for Sale in Japan" received special commendation from anti-trafficking organizations for raising awareness about child exploitation. Similar recognition came from mental health advocacy groups following her sensitive coverage of psychiatric care facilities.

The television industry's respect manifested through prime-time broadcasting slots and increased commissioning of her work. Major networks competed for her projects, recognizing both their journalistic merit and audience appeal. This professional recognition translated into greater creative freedom and resources for tackling challenging subjects.

Educational institutions began incorporating her documentaries into journalism and media studies curricula. Universities cited her work as exemplary examples of contemporary documentary making, studying her techniques for combining serious journalism with engaging presentation styles.

Publishing success added another dimension to her professional achievements. Her debut book reached Sunday Times bestseller status, expanding her influence beyond broadcasting to print media. This accomplishment demonstrated her ability to translate television success into other formats.

The British Academy of Film and Television Arts (BAFTA) recognized her contributions through various nominations and special mentions. Though not always resulting in wins, these acknowledgments from Britain's premier entertainment organization reflected industry-wide respect for her work.

International recognition came through numerous festival selections and awards. Her documentaries regularly featured in prestigious documentary film festivals worldwide, spreading her influence beyond British borders. Foreign broadcasters increasingly sought rights to air her programs, expanding her global impact.

Professional journalism organizations praised her dedication to maintaining ethical standards while covering controversial subjects. The National Union of Journalists highlighted her work as an example of responsible reporting on sensitive issues.

Her achievement in winning Strictly Come Dancing, while not directly related to journalism, demonstrated her versatility as a broadcaster and public figure. This victory increased her visibility while maintaining her credibility as a serious journalist.

Recognition from advocacy groups acknowledged her role in bringing attention to crucial social issues. Organizations working with vulnerable populations particularly appreciated her sensitive approach to difficult subjects.

Media industry publications regularly featured her work in their "best of" lists and retrospectives. Trade journals cited her influence on changing approaches to documentary presentation and subject matter.

Professional development programs incorporated study of her techniques into their training materials. New journalists learned from her examples of building trust with subjects while maintaining professional standards.

Her achievements inspired similar programs focusing on social issues and investigative journalism. Other broadcasters sought to replicate her successful combination of serious content with accessible presentation styles.

The breadth of her professional recognition spans multiple aspects of media work. From hard-hitting documentaries to entertainment programs, her versatility earned respect across broadcasting genres.

Youth organizations particularly celebrated her example of achievement through determination and authenticity. Her story inspired young people from similar backgrounds to pursue careers in media and journalism.

The impact of her work prompted academic studies examining her influence on contemporary documentary making. Researchers analyzed her techniques for making complex subjects accessible to general audiences.

Professional mentoring programs sought her participation, recognizing her value as a role model for emerging journalists. Her experience transitioning from subject to presenter offered unique insights for aspiring broadcasters.

Industry conferences regularly featured her work as case studies in effective documentary making. Her methods for building trust with subjects while maintaining journalistic standards provided valuable lessons for media professionals.

Environmental organizations commended her coverage of sustainability issues, particularly her investigations into fashion industry pollution. These acknowledgments highlighted her role in bringing attention to crucial environmental concerns.

Her achievements contributed to changing perceptions of what constitutes effective documentary presentation. Traditional journalism organizations came to appreciate her more informal but equally rigorous approach to serious subjects.

The range of her professional recognition reflects both depth and breadth of impact. From royal honors to grassroots acknowledgments, her work resonated across social and professional boundaries.

Recognition continued building through each phase of her career development. Each new project added fresh dimensions to her professional reputation while maintaining core journalistic values.

The cumulative effect of these honors established her as a significant voice in contemporary broadcasting. Her achievements helped create new standards for combining serious journalism with popular appeal.

Professional respect translated into opportunities for innovation in format and subject matter. Her proven track record enabled exploration of new approaches to documentary making and presentation.

The diversity of recognition highlighted her success in reaching multiple audiences while maintaining professional standards.

Key Highlights

1. Stacey Dooley's appointment as Member of the Order of the British Empire (MBE) in the 2018 Birthday Honours marked the pinnacle of recognition for her services to broadcasting, symbolizing her extraordinary journey from shop assistant to respected journalist.

2. Her documentary work gained significant industry recognition, particularly "Face to Face with ISIS," winning the Popular Features category at the One World Media Awards while consistently breaking BBC Three viewership records on iPlayer.

3. Beyond broadcasting, her influence extended into print media with a Sunday Times bestseller, while educational institutions incorporated her work into

journalism curricula, recognizing her unique approach to documentary making.

4. The breadth of professional recognition spans multiple fields, from BAFTA nominations to international festival selections, establishing her as a significant voice in contemporary broadcasting while maintaining credibility across both serious journalism and entertainment.

Reflection Questions

1. How does Stacey's journey from shop assistant to MBE recipient challenge our perceptions of traditional career paths in journalism?

2. What role has her unique documentary style played in earning both critical acclaim and popular success?

3. How has formal recognition of her work influenced the broader field of documentary making?

_____
_____
_____
_____
_____

4. Why do you think Stacey's achievements resonate across such a wide range of audiences and institutions?

_____
_____
_____
_____
_____

CHAPTER 7

LEGACY AND IMPACT

"The real purpose of journalism is to raise public awareness of what really matters in our world."
Walter Cronkite

Stacey Dooley's influence on British broadcasting extends far beyond her personal achievements. Her unique approach to documentary making has reshaped how serious subjects reach mainstream audiences, creating a legacy that continues influencing new generations of journalists and filmmakers.

The transformation of documentary presentation stands among her most significant contributions to broadcasting. By combining thorough investigation with accessible delivery, she demonstrated that serious journalism need not sacrifice mass appeal. This balance created new possibilities for engaging younger audiences with complex social issues.

Her impact on BBC Three proved particularly significant, helping establish the channel's reputation for meaningful content despite its youth-oriented focus. The success of her documentaries showed that young audiences would engage with serious subjects when presented authentically and respectfully.

Broadcasting techniques developed through her work have become industry standards. Her direct, conversational interview style broke down traditional barriers between presenter and subject, creating more intimate and revealing documentaries. This approach influenced a new generation of documentary makers seeking to connect with contemporary audiences.

The integration of social media and digital platforms with traditional broadcasting demonstrated her understanding of changing media consumption patterns. Her ability to maintain professional standards while adapting to new formats provided a model for broadcasters navigating technological change.

Documentary journalism particularly benefited from her innovations in storytelling techniques. By prioritizing human connections over formal presentation, she created more engaging and impactful programs. This style proved especially effective when covering challenging or controversial subjects.

Her influence on investigative journalism showed through increased attention to ethical representation and subject dignity. The controversies she faced led to improved industry practices regarding fact-checking and representation of vulnerable individuals.

Young journalists frequently cite her work as inspiration for their own career choices. Her journey from participant to presenter demonstrated possible pathways to broadcasting for those without traditional media backgrounds. This legacy continues encouraging diverse voices in journalism.

Social issue awareness significantly increased through her documentary work. Programs covering child labor, sex trafficking, and environmental destruction brought these issues to mainstream attention. Her ability to make complex problems understandable while maintaining their urgency helped mobilize public response.

The impact on mental health awareness stands out among her contributions. Documentary coverage of psychiatric facilities and mental health challenges helped reduce stigma while increasing public understanding. These programs continue influencing discussions about mental healthcare access and support.

Environmental consciousness grew through her investigations of fashion industry pollution and sustainable practices. These documentaries connected everyday consumer choices with global environmental impact, encouraging more responsible purchasing decisions.

Gender equality benefited from her consistent focus on women's experiences worldwide. By highlighting both challenges and achievements, her work contributed to broader understanding of gender-based issues across cultures.

Youth empowerment remained central to her legacy through programs addressing challenges facing young people globally. From education access to economic opportunity, these documentaries helped amplify youth voices on crucial issues.

Her influence on charitable sector practices prompted important changes in representation and storytelling. The Comic Relief controversy led to broader discussions about dignity and agency in international development narratives.

Broadcasting education evolved partly due to her impact on documentary techniques. Media schools now study her methods for combining journalistic rigor with accessible presentation. Her work provides practical examples of effective contemporary documentary making.

Professional standards in international reporting improved through lessons learned from her experiences. Industry guidelines now emphasize careful verification and cultural sensitivity when covering stories across borders.

The democratization of documentary making owes much to her example. By showing that authentic storytelling could succeed without formal journalism training, she helped open the field to diverse voices and perspectives.

Her legacy includes improved understanding of complex global issues among younger audiences. By making serious subjects accessible without oversimplification, she helped build more informed and engaged viewers.

The impact on public discourse about social issues continues growing through her body of work. Programs covering controversial subjects often spark important discussions about societal challenges and potential solutions.

Documentary production practices changed significantly under her influence. Greater emphasis on subject dignity and ethical storytelling reflects lessons learned through her career experiences.

Her contribution to breaking down class barriers in broadcasting remains significant. Her success demonstrated that talent and determination could overcome traditional industry limitations.

The evolution of presenter-led documentaries owes much to her pioneering style. Personal engagement with subjects while maintaining professional standards created new possibilities for documentary formats.

Social media engagement in documentary promotion developed partly through her example. Strategic use of digital platforms to extend program impact provided models for contemporary broadcasters.

Industry recognition of different storytelling approaches expanded through her success. Traditional journalism increasingly accepts more personal, engaged presentation styles while maintaining professional standards.

Her influence on representation in media continues growing as new generations enter broadcasting. Diverse voices find encouragement in her example of authentic storytelling and professional achievement.

The lasting impact on public awareness of social issues demonstrates the effectiveness of her approach. Complex problems become more understandable through human-centered storytelling without losing their urgency or importance.

Broadcasting's future partly reflects her legacy of combining serious content with accessible presentation. New generations of documentary makers build on her innovations while developing their own voices.

Her contribution to contemporary journalism extends beyond specific techniques to fundamental questions about purpose and responsibility. The balance between informing and engaging audiences remains central to her legacy in broadcasting.

The evolution of documentary journalism continues reflecting her influence through emphasis on human connection and ethical storytelling. Future developments will likely build on foundations she helped establish.

Her impact on social issue awareness continues to grow through the ongoing influence of her work. New audiences discover her documentaries while current viewers apply their insights to emerging challenges.

Key Highlights

1. Stacey Dooley revolutionized documentary presentation by successfully combining serious investigative journalism with accessible delivery, proving that complex social issues could engage mainstream audiences, particularly younger viewers, through BBC Three.

2. Her unique interviewing style and emphasis on human connection created new standards in documentary journalism, influencing industry practices in ethical representation, fact-checking, and the treatment of vulnerable subjects.

3. Through her documentaries, she significantly increased public awareness of crucial social issues ranging from mental health and environmental concerns to gender equality and child labor, making complex

global problems understandable without diminishing their urgency.

4. Her journey from participant to presenter helped democratize broadcasting by demonstrating that authentic storytelling and determination could overcome traditional industry barriers, inspiring a new generation of diverse voices in journalism.

Reflection Questions

1. How has Stacey's approach to documentary making changed the way we engage with serious social issues on television?

   _____
   _____
   _____
   _____
   _____
   _____

2. What makes her presenting style so effective at connecting with younger audiences while maintaining journalistic integrity?

   _____
   _____
   _____
   _____
   _____
   _____

3. How might her legacy influence the next generation of documentary makers and journalists?

4. Why do you think her journey from participant to presenter resonates so strongly with aspiring broadcasters?

CHAPTER 8

FILMOGRAPHY

"Television is not just a job; it is a creative medium for storytelling that touches millions of lives."
Barbara Walters

The screen presence of Stacey Dooley spans more than fifteen years, creating a diverse portfolio that showcases her versatility and evolution as a broadcaster. Her filmography tells the story of a natural talent who transformed from participant to presenter, from investigator to entertainer.

2008 introduced viewers to an unknown Stacey Dooley through "Blood, Sweat, and T-shirts." The four-part series placed her alongside other young British fashion consumers in Indian garment factories. Her authentic reactions and genuine interest in workers' lives distinguished her from fellow participants, catching the attention of BBC producers.

BBC Three recognized her potential and launched "Stacey Dooley Investigates" in 2009. The series became her flagship program, running for multiple seasons and covering an impressive range of social issues. From child labor to drug trafficking, from war zones to environmental crises, each episode demonstrated her growing confidence and journalistic skill.

"Tourism and the Truth" (2011) expanded her investigative scope, examining the hidden costs of global tourism in Thailand and Kenya. The two-part series revealed her ability to handle complex economic and social issues while maintaining audience engagement.

Her work with younger audiences through CBBC's "Show Me What You're Made Of" displayed her adaptability across different viewing demographics. The series, which ran from 2011 to 2017, proved she could communicate effectively with children while handling serious subjects.

2012 brought personal challenge and professional growth with "My Hometown Fanatics," filmed in Luton. The documentary required careful balance between personal connection and professional objectivity while investigating extremism in her hometown.

"Coming Here Soon" (2012) took her to Greece, Ireland, and Japan to explore the impact of the global financial crisis on young people. Though the Japan episode drew criticism for its coverage of suicide, it demonstrated her willingness to tackle difficult subjects.

The "USA Series" (2012-2014) expanded her international profile, investigating issues affecting American teenagers. Topics ranged from gun violence to homelessness, showing her ability to connect with young people across cultural boundaries.

"Sex in Strange Places" (2016) examined different cultural approaches to sexuality and sex work. The series showcased her maturing approach to sensitive subjects, though the Turkish episode later faced criticism for misidentification.

Reality television provided new opportunities for growth. Her 2018 participation in "strictly come dancing" revealed her competitive spirit and determination. Partnership with Kevin Clifton led to victory and dramatically increased her public profile.

"Glow Up: Britain's Next Make-Up Star" (2019-2020) showcased her skills as an entertainment presenter. The competition series demonstrated her ability to balance encouraging contestants while maintaining professional standards.

Guest appearances on shows like "RuPaul's Drag Race UK" (2019) and "Have I Got News for You" revealed her comfort with entertainment formats. These appearances helped broaden her appeal while maintaining her credibility as a serious journalist.

"Stacey Dooley Sleeps Over" (2019-present) created a unique documentary format, embedding herself in unusual households. The series demonstrated her ability to innovate while maintaining focus on human stories.

"EastEnders: Secrets from the Square" (2020) proved her versatility during pandemic restrictions. Presenting behind-the-scenes content for Britain's popular soap opera showed her adaptability to different broadcasting challenges.

"DNA Family Secrets" (2021) partnered her with geneticist Turi King, combining science with human interest stories. The series showcased her ability to make complex subjects accessible while handling emotional revelations sensitively.

Participation in celebrity game shows like "The Masked Dancer" (2022) and "Celebrity Catchphrase" displayed her willingness to embrace pure entertainment. These appearances helped maintain public visibility while working on serious documentaries.

Her television specials consistently tackled challenging subjects. "Two Daughters" (2022) and "Inside the Convent" (2022) demonstrated her continuing commitment to diverse storytelling approaches.

Documentary specials like "Stalkers" and "Ready for War?" highlighted her ongoing dedication to investigative journalism. These programs maintained her reputation for tackling serious subjects while reaching broad audiences.

Guest hosting on "The One Show" and appearances on "Loose Women" proved her capability in live television formats. These opportunities showcased her quick thinking and natural rapport with co-presenters.

Reality competition appearances on "The Great Celebrity Bake Off" and "Celebrity Lingo" revealed her sporting nature and ability to connect with audiences through entertainment formats.

Panel show appearances on "Would I Lie to You?" and "Have I Got News for You" demonstrated her quick wit and ability to engage in light-hearted entertainment while maintaining professional dignity.

Her consistent presence across BBC channels showed versatility in handling different broadcasting styles and audience expectations. From serious documentaries to light entertainment, she maintained authenticity across formats.

Special documentary projects allowed deeper exploration of specific issues. Programs focusing on mental health, crime, and social justice demonstrated her continuing commitment to serious journalism.

Regular appearances on entertainment shows balanced her documentary work, creating a rounded public persona that appealed to diverse audiences. This variety prevented typecasting while maintaining professional credibility.

Guest appearances on discussion programs provided platforms for sharing insights from her documentary work. These opportunities allowed her to reach new audiences with important social messages.

International broadcast sales of her documentaries expanded her influence beyond British television. Global audiences connected with her direct, honest approach to investigating complex issues.

Reality show participation revealed different aspects of her personality while maintaining professional standards. Each appearance strengthened her position as a versatile broadcaster capable of handling various formats.

Documentary series remained the core of her television work, establishing new standards for combining serious journalism with accessible presentation. Her influence on contemporary documentary making continues to grow through pioneering new approaches to storytelling.

Her filmography demonstrates remarkable range and consistent growth as a broadcaster. From participant to presenter, from investigator to entertainer, each project contributed to developing a unique television presence.

The breadth of her television work creates a comprehensive picture of contemporary broadcasting. Her career spans significant changes in television production and consumption, adapting successfully to evolving audience expectations.

EPILOGUE

Stacey Dooley's remarkable journey from a shop assistant in Luton to one of Britain's most respected documentary makers exemplifies the power of authenticity, determination, and genuine curiosity about the human experience. Her story transcends traditional narratives of success, demonstrating that true impact comes not just from personal achievements but from the ability to connect, illuminate, and inspire change.

Through her distinctive approach to documentary journalism, Dooley has transformed how serious subjects reach mainstream audiences.

Her work consistently bridges the gap between complex social issues and public understanding, making crucial conversations accessible without diminishing their importance.

The evolution of her career from participant to presenter, from investigator to influential broadcaster, charts a path that has redefined possibilities in contemporary media.

Her personal growth parallels her professional development. The relationship with Kevin Clifton, journey into motherhood, and continuous advocacy for social causes reveal a public figure who maintains authenticity while navigating fame's challenges. These experiences have enriched her perspective, deepening the empathy and understanding she brings to her documentary work.

The controversies and challenges she faced became opportunities for industry-wide learning and improvement. Her responses to criticism demonstrated both resilience and willingness to engage with difficult conversations about representation and responsibility in media. These experiences contributed to positive changes in how broadcasters approach international reporting and charitable campaigns.

Recognition through awards, including her MBE, validates not just personal achievement but the importance of authentic storytelling in contemporary journalism. Her success has opened doors for diverse voices in broadcasting, proving that talent and dedication can overcome traditional industry barriers.

The legacy Stacey Dooley creates extends beyond her impressive filmography. Her influence shapes how future generations approach documentary making, social advocacy, and public engagement with important issues. Most significantly, she demonstrates that maintaining genuine curiosity and compassion while pursuing professional excellence creates lasting positive impact.

Stacey Dooley's story reminds us that greatness often comes not from following established paths but from forging new ones with courage, integrity, and unwavering commitment to illuminating truth. Her journey continues inspiring those who seek to make meaningful contributions through media, proving that authentic voices can indeed change how we see and understand our world.

Printed in Great Britain
by Amazon